THE SELF-IMAGE OF A CHRISTIAN

The Living as a Christian series:

Basic Christian Maturity

Growing in Faith
   Steve Clark

Knowing God's Will
   Steve Clark

Decision to Love
What It Means to Love Others from the Heart
   Ken Wilson

God First
What It Means to Love God above All Things
   Ken Wilson

The Emotions

The Angry Christian
How to Control—and Use—Your Anger
   Bert Ghezzi

The Self-Image of a Christian
Humility and Self-Esteem
   Mark Kinzer

Bert Ghezzi and Peter Williamson
General Editors

The Self-Image of a Christian

Humility and Self-Esteem

Mark Kinzer

Servant Books
Ann Arbor, Michigan

Copyright © 1980 by Mark Kinzer
All rights reserved.
Published by Servant Books, Box 8617,
Ann Arbor, Michigan 48107

Book design and cover photo by John B. Leidy,
© copyright 1980 Servant Publications

Printed in the United States of America

ISBN 0-89283-088-3

Contents

Series Introduction / 7
Preface / 13

1. False Humility / 15
2. Think with Sober Judgment / 27
3. Timidity / 43
4. True Humility: The Mind of a Servant / 55
5. Jesus, the Perfect Model of Humility / 71
6. Overcoming Problems of Self-Image / 83
7. The Goal: Freedom and Servanthood / 101

SERIES INTRODUCTION

Living as a Christian

In human terms, it is not easy to decide to follow Jesus Christ and to live our lives as Christians. Jesus requires that we surrender our selves to him, relinquish our aspirations for our lives, and submit our will to God. Men and women have never been able to do this easily; if we could, we wouldn't need a savior.

Once we accept the invitation and decide to follow Jesus, a new set of obstacles and problems assert themselves. We find that we are often ignorant about what God wants of us as his sons and daughters. For example, what does it mean practically to obey the first commandment — to love God with our whole mind, heart, and strength? How can we know God's will? How do we love people we don't like? How does being a Christian affect what we do with our time and money? What does it mean "to turn the other cheek?" In these areas — and many others — it is not easy to understand exactly what God wants.

Even when we do know what God wants, it can be quite difficult to apply his teaching to our daily lives. Questions abound. How do we find time to pray regularly? How do we repair a relationship with someone we have wronged or who has wronged us? How do we handle unruly emotional reactions?

These are examples of perplexing questions about the application of Christian teaching to our daily lives.

Furthermore, we soon discover that Christians have enemies — the devil outside and the flesh within. Satan tempts us to sin; our inner urges welcome the temptation, and we find our will to resist steadily eroding.

Finally, we must overcome the world. We are trying to live in an environment that is hostile toward what Christians believe and how they live and friendly toward those who believe and do the opposite. The world in which we live works on our Christian resolve in many subtle ways. How much easier it is to think and act like those around us! How do we persevere?

There is a two-fold answer to these questions: To live successfully as Christians, we need both grace and wisdom. Both are freely available from the Lord to those who seek him.

As Christians we live by grace. The very life of God works in us as we try to understand God's teaching, apply it to our lives, and overcome the forces that would turn us aside from our chosen path. We never stand in need of grace. It is always there. The Lord is with us always, and the supply of his grace is inexhaustible.

Yet grace works with wisdom. Christians must *learn* a great deal about how to live according to God's will. We must study God's word in scripture, listen to Christian teaching, and reflect on our own experience and the experience of others. Many Christians today lack this kind of wisdom. This is the need which the *Living as a Christian* series is designed to meet.

The book you are reading is part of a series of books intended to help Christians apply the teaching of scripture to their lives. The authors of *Living as a Christian* books are pastoral leaders who have given this teaching in programs of Christian formation in various Christian communities. The teaching has stood the test of time. It has already helped many people grow as faithful servants of the Lord. We decided it was time to make this teaching available in book form.

All the *Living as a Christian* books seek to meet the following criteria:

- **Biblical.** The teaching is rooted in scripture. The authors and editors maintain that scripture is the word of God, and that it ought to determine what Christians believe and how they live.

- **Practical.** The purpose of the series is to offer down-to-earth advice about living as a Christian.

- **Relevant.** The teaching is aimed at the needs we encounter in our daily lives — at home, in school, on the job, in our day-to-day relationships.

- **Brief and Readable.** We have designed the series for busy people from a wide variety of backgrounds. Each of the authors presents profound Christian truths as simply and clearly as possible, and illustrates those truths by examples drawn from personal experience.

- **Integrated.** The books in the series comprise a unified curriculum on Christian living. They do not present differing views, but rather they take a consistent approach.

The format of the series makes it suitable for both individual and group use. The books in *Living as a Christian* can be used in such group settings as Sunday school classes, adult education programs, prayer groups, classes for teen-agers, women's groups, and as a supplement to Bible study.

The *Living as a Christian* series is divided into several sets of books, each devoted to a different aspect of Christian living. These sets include books on Christian maturity, emotions in the Christian life, the fruit of the Holy Spirit, Christian personal relationships, Christian service, and very likely, on other topics as well.

This book, *The Self-Image of a Christian*, is part of a set covering the emotions in the Christian life. The nature of modern society forces us to be more concerned about our emotions than our Christian ancestors had to be. Not that they were unemotional. Ironically, they were more expressive of their emotions than most of us are. But nowadays we look at our emotions differently, and the instability of relationships and pressures of modern life introduce some new problems. *The Self-Image of a Christian* and other books in this set present a practical scripturally based strategy for emotional health.

The editors dedicate the *Living as a Christian* series to Christian men and women everywhere who have counted the cost and decided to follow Jesus Christ as his disciples.

Bert Ghezzi and Peter Williamson
General Editors

Preface

Many of us today struggle against feelings of fear, insecurity, and self-deprecation. We doubt our abilities and our basic worth as people. To be sure, these feelings become serious emotional disorders in only a few of us. However, most of us know how emotional insecurity and a poor self-image can weaken our capacity to confidently and freely serve others.

One would think that being a Christian would eliminate problems of self-image. After all, God has revealed his love for us in Christ, and has poured that love into our hearts through the Holy Spirit. We are sons and daughters of God. How can we question our basic worth? How can we yield to discouragement and fear? The power and love of God should bring us to greater freedom and confidence as his sons and daughters.

Nevertheless, Christians do yield to discouragement and fear. Many of us have weak—even negative—images of ourselves.

One reason is a common misunderstanding of an aspect of Christian teaching—the teaching on humility. Does not Christ teach us to despise ourselves and look upon all others as better than ourselves? Should we not strive to be retiring and quiet, seen and heard as little as possible? Isn't it a Christian virtue to think poorly of oneself? This view of humility can produce the very emotional problem we are trying to overcome.

The truth is that this view of humility is not the Christian teaching at all. A false notion of Christian humility will encourage us to feel bad about ourselves, to doubt our basic worth, and to avoid bold, confident, aggressive action. A true notion of Christian humility will free us to act with the kind of holy boldness seen in the lives of such men as Jesus and the Apostle Paul.

In this short book, I would like to do three things to help Christians grow in freedom and confidence: (1) to define Christian humility and distinguish it clearly from feeling bad about ourselves or being timid; (2) to describe what our self-image should be as Christians; and (3) to offer some practical advice on how to overcome problems deriving from a poor self-image. The Lord wants us to be humble and to know our own self-worth. He wants us to take on the self-image of a servant.

ONE

False Humility

Do nothing from selfishness or conceit, but in humility count others better than yourselves. Phil 2:3

A good friend of mine read this passage soon after his conversion to Christianity. He was a zealous young disciple, and he wanted to obey the full teaching of scripture. The teaching in this passage seemed to him clear enough: be humble and count others better than yourself. Therefore, he resolved to regard everyone better than himself. As he encountered other people in the course of his daily tasks, he would say to himself, "This person is better than me, that person is better than me, all of these people are better than me."

After a short time my friend became disillusioned with these humility-drills. First of all, he did not genuinely believe he was such a wretched person. He knew his failings, his weaknesses, and his sins, but he could not believe that he was the worst person in the world. Secondly, he encountered several people who by any objective standard did not appear to be better than him. My friend did not glory in his moral superiority like the Pharisee in Luke 18:9-14, nor presume to know fully what was in peoples' hearts; still, it was difficult to pretend that every non-Christian he met enjoyed a better standing with God than he did. Finally, he noticed that he was spending more time than ever before thinking about himself and comparing himself to other people. "Something must be wrong with my interpretation of this scripture passage," he concluded. He then prudently chose to set the passage aside until he received further illumination.

My friend's interpretation of Philippians 2 is one that is all too common among Christians. According to this view, being humble means having a low opinion of yourself, feeling bad about yourself, thinking of yourself as inferior to others. "I'm the worst person of all" should thus be the self-evaluation of the truly humble man.

Is this really the attitude of the truly humble man? A thoughtful reading of the scripture indicates that this understanding falls far short of true Christian humility. True humility should free us from all preoccupation with ourselves, whereas a low self-opinion tends to focus our attention on ourselves. C.S. Lewis notes this difference between true and false humility in *Mere Christianity*:

> Do not imagine that if you meet a really humble man he will be what most people call "humble" nowadays: He will not be a sort of greasy, swarmy person, who is always telling you that, of course, he is nobody. Probably all you will think about him is that he seemed a cheerful, intelligent chap who took a real interest in what

you said to *him*. If you do dislike him, it will be because you feel a little envious of anyone who seems to enjoy life so easily. He will not be thinking about humility: he will not be thinking about himself at all.

There is a great difference between "a really humble man" and "what most people call 'humble' nowadays." To feel bad about yourself and maintain the lowest possible self-opinion is not the definition of true Christian humility.

Low Self-Worth—An Emotional Problem

The view that humility means having a low opinion of oneself can also feed an emotional problem experienced by many people in our society: lack of self-respect, self-worth, and self-confidence. Early in my life as a Christian I dismissed these problems as being insignificant. It seemed to me then that most modern people have a more than healthy dose of pride and self-love. However, years of pastoral experience have convinced me that this opinion was too hasty and superficial. Problems with low self-worth and lack of confidence are more subtle, widespread, and harmful than I had first acknowledged.

As a pastor serving in a Christian community of highly committed people, I have had many opportunities to talk frankly with people about difficulties they are experiencing. When I first began serving in this way, I was immediately surprised to discover how many people are plagued by self-doubt and insecurity. In fact, this was probably the most common difficulty I encountered in the people I cared for. After a few years of experience as a pastor, I also began to see connections between low self-worth and many other problems that had previously seemed unrelated to it. Low self-worth was often at the root of obstacles as diverse as weight difficulties, personality conflicts, and sexual problems.

One young man in our community approached me for help in overcoming a difficulty he was having with uncontrolled eating habits. As he described his difficulty, I began to see a connection between it and another difficulty I knew he had with anxiety and lack of confidence. The two problems fit together neatly. He found an outlet for his anxiety by overeating; at the same time, his lack of confidence gave him the firm conviction that he would be unable to control his eating habits. I decided not to admonish this young man for his failure to master his appetites, but instead I encouraged him and tried to impart confidence to him. My intention was to relieve his anxiety and to bolster his confidence that he could in fact grow in self-control. This strategy seemed to succeed. He has grown in confidence, and he has mastered the eating problem that so concerned him.

Experiences like this enabled me to see and handle the problems many people have with lack of self-confidence and self-worth, but of course I never suspected that this was a problem for me. If anything, my difficulties and defects were in the other direction—an excess of confidence, self-assurance, and pride. I had always succeeded marvelously at school, and never lacked close friends. I was aggressively outspoken in my opinions, and welcomed the challenge of a good argument. I was a perfectionist in my work—if Mark Kinzer did it, then it would be done well. I also entertained grand ambitions for my future. Who could foretell what great position I might attain, what great achievement I might win? All seemed within my reach.

When I first became a Christian, it was clear to me that I needed to renounce my former pride, perfectionism, and ambition. For several years I struggled against these tendencies, repenting time and time again. Finally, an older Christian man of proven wisdom advised me that my problem might be more than just a matter of ambition and pride. "I think that you suffer from a lack of confidence and an excessive desire for approval and reassurance," he concluded. This insight startled me. Could my energetic striving for position and excellence be attributed in part to a desire to prove myself? As I thought about my life, I realized that this was the case. Not only did I need to repent of ambition—I also needed to grow in my understanding of who I was as a son of God who had no need to prove himself to his Father.

Aggressive striving for approval is only one of many common manifestations of a basic problem with low self-worth and lack of confidence. Another common manifestation is depression. Many of us fall occasionally into states of depression where we feel bad about ourselves and feel convinced that no one loves us or respects us. This type of self-pity is often connected to an underlying problem with low self-worth. We feel that our problem comes from the objective fact that we are worth little or nothing and are not valued by others; in fact, the problem comes from our accepting this illusory feeling as an accurate view of reality.

Another manifestation of low self-worth is defensiveness—a difficulty in receiving correction when we have made mistakes. Most of us respond to correction with some defensiveness. Some of this response is simply human pride; few of us are ever glad to find out we are wrong. However, defensiveness is sometimes rooted in a shaky sense of self-worth. Many of us have a heavy emotional investment in being right. We do not take our own worth for granted, and being right helps us to establish our worth. Thus, when we are wrong and someone corrects us, we take it as a reflection on our value as a human being, and we respond defensively. In such cases, defensiveness is a sign of insecurity and lack of a sense of self-worth.

I found such a connection between defensiveness and insecurity in another young man in my Christian community. He was one of the most broadly knowledgeable and generally competent people I had ever known. As our acquaintance deepened, I began to notice some peculiar features in his response to correction: Upon hearing that he had made a mistake, his face and body would tighten with tension, and he would then attempt to evade responsibility for the mistake. I also noticed a similar pattern of behavior when he tried to speak personally about his weaknesses and limitations. His usually cheerful brow would mat with tension and his ordinarily articulate conversation would become vague and evasive.

After witnessing these patterns on several occasions, I became convinced that this man suffered from a problem with insecurity that he had probably never acknowledged. I decided to raise the issue with him. As we talked, it became obvious that my hunch was correct. He had always drawn security from his knowledge and competence; whenever these were called into question he became irrationally anxious and tried to prove that he was right. For years he had refused to acknowledge his own weaknesses and limitations because their presence reinforced his sense of insecurity. This insight into the root of his defensiveness both helped this man respond differently to correction, mistakes, and personal weaknesses, and also led to his being strengthened in other areas of his life.

A very different problem experienced by many Christians is an inability to receive praise and encouragement. This too may be a manifestation of low self-worth. Of course other factors can also lead us to resist encouragement—for example, an independent spirit or a particular view of humility (a false view, as we shall see later). However, many people feel uncomfortable about receiving words of praise and encouragement because they believe that these words must be inaccurate and unjustified. "He's just trying to be nice," we think, or, "She's just trying to make me feel good." We say these things because the praise of others does not fit our own low estimation of ourselves. Thus, the same emotional difficulty that leads us to resist correction for our real mistakes also leads us to resist praise for our real strengths, gifts, and virtues.

I have a Christian friend who combines in his personality both low self-esteem and a will of granite. Both characteristics are revealed in his steadfast resistance to praise and encouragement. He is a man of many talents, as well as a man of fine Christian character. However, he refuses to accept the praise he receives even from those he most respects. Instead, he clings to his own low estimation of his character and his abilities. If he were to receive more freely the encouragement of his brothers, he would undoubtedly grow in the confidence that is lacking in many areas of his life.

Another emotional problem often connected to low self-worth is self-condemnation. Many Christians experience severe guilt feelings far out of proportion to the wrongdoing they actually commit. We not only doubt our value and abilities; we also see ourselves as morally corrupt. The question of guilt feelings is a complicated pastoral issue, since these feelings are sometimes signs of genuine wrongdoing that needs to be repented of. I do not want to treat here at any length the topic of self-condemnation and moral unworthiness. However, it is helpful to note that self-condemnation is sometimes related to a problem with low self-worth.

Sources of the Problem

When I was a young Christian, I was suspicious of the emphasis some people place on the problem of low self-worth because I noticed that scripture gives little emphasis to it. Scriptural teaching is clearly more concerned with pride, ambition, and independence than it is with lack of confidence. Why is this the case?

The reason, I have concluded, is that the social structure taught and presumed in scripture differs greatly from the social structure of our own modern society. As the nature of social groupings change, so does the nature of social and psychological problems people experience within them. Many of the problems that we find most pressing—addiction, adolescent alienation, marital instability, psychological maladjustment—are either ignored in the scripture or given little attention. The problem with low self-worth appears to fall within this category of special modern problems that were less significant in scriptural times. We can fruitfully apply scriptural principles to these modern problems, but we cannot pretend that the writers of scripture saw them as "problems" in the same way we do.

What specific changes in social structure explain the greater modern problem with low self-worth? Many complex factors are certainly involved. However, three social changes are particularly important: First, the weakening of the family; second, the breakdown of wider kinship groupings and stable neighborhood clusters; third, the increasing importance of peer groupings.

The first social change that has aggravated problems with low self-worth is the weakening of the family unit. Most modern families have significantly less discipline, commitment, and stability than did families in scriptural times. This affects individual self-worth because the family is the most powerful formative influence on human personality development. Stable, committed families usually produce more secure and confident children, whereas weaker families produce children with less confidence. From this point of view, then, it is understandable that individuals in a society with a strong and healthy family structure will have fewer problems with self-worth than individuals in a society that suffers from severe family disorder. Therefore, the deterioration of modern family life probably bears large responsibility for our special modern problems with self-worth.

Second, many of the same social forces that have weakened the family have also eroded wider kinship groupings and neighborhood clusters. Young men and women growing up in Jesus' day spent most of their early life around family members—brothers, sisters, parents, cousins, aunts, uncles. Others who lived nearby would be related to almost like family members. Education, entertainment, and work all took place within committed personal realtionships. These groupings gave considerable emotional support and relieved young men and women from much of the pressure to "earn approval." By contrast, men and women today must constantly prove themselves in the impersonal school and work environments which have replaced the traditional groupings. The constant evaluation which must take place in these impersonal settings can easily provoke insecurity, fear of failure, and chronic need for approval. Thus, the general shift in society from committed personal groupings (such as kinship and neighborhood groups) to more impersonal institutional settings has probably increased our modern problems with self-worth.

Third, the rising power of peer groups has probably also heightened our modern emotional conflicts. In Jesus' day, peer groups were not as important as they are today. Peer groups provide some emotional support for their members, but they also usually involve a fierce fight to gain approval, to be accepted, to "belong." I recall vividly the peer group pressures exerted on myself and others during my high school years. It seemed terribly important to be "in" with a group of people who were themselves "in" with other groups of people. Inevitably, a good many people were clearly "out." However, even those who were "in" needed to fight to stay "in." This mad quest for peer acceptance formed the rules for high school survival. It is not surprising to witness the outcome in the lives of many people: insecurity, fear of losing or not gaining acceptance, and a basic sense of low self-worth.

Problems with self-worth may not have been totally absent in scriptural times. However, it does seem as though our modern society is afflicted with these problems in a unique way. Whatever historical changes underlie this distinctive modern affliction, we are still faced with a modern problem which we cannot afford to ignore—a problem with the way in which we look at ourselves.

False Humility and Low Self-Worth

The Christian view of humility has often been confused with having a low self-evaluation. This misunderstanding can be very dangerous for Christians who have a problem with low self-worth. What is actually an emotional problem disguises itself as a spiritual virtue. Therefore, the next questions that arise are these: How should Christians look at themselves? What is Christian humility?

TWO

Think With Sober Judgment

What does scripture teach us about how we should look at ourselves? We can find the answer to this question in a single verse in the twelfth chapter of Romans:

> For by the grace given to me I bid every one among you not to think of himself more highly than he ought to think, but to *think with sober judgment*, each according to the measure of faith which God has assigned him. (Rom 12:3 Emphasis added)

What does Paul mean when he teaches us to hold an opinion of ourselves based on "sober judgment?" The Greek word he uses can also be translated as "clear-minded," "reasonable," "sensible," or "moderate." To think with "sober judgment" is to think accurately and truthfully, without yielding to unreasonable influences or unjustified extremes. Thus the scriptural teaching on this point is simpler than we might have expected: We should see ourselves as truthfully and accurately as possible.

God wants us to entertain a *truthful* opinion of

ourselves, not a *low* opinion. C.S. Lewis makes this point with great humor and force in a passage from *The Screwtape Letters*. Screwtape is a senior demon in Hell writing to his nephew, Wormwood, a junior tempter in need of instruction. The "patient" is the man whom Wormwood is currently tempting. Screwtape writes:

> You must therefore conceal from the patient the true end of Humility. Let him think of it, not as self-forgetfulness, but as a certain kind of opinion (namely, a low opinion) of his own talents and character. Some talents, I gather, he really has. Fix in his mind the idea that humility consists in trying to believe those talents to be less valuable than he believes them to be. No doubt they are in fact less valuable than he believes, but that is not the point. The great thing is to make him value an opinion for some quality other than *truth*, thus introducing an element of dishonesty and make-believe into the heart of what otherwise threatens to become a virtue. By this method thousands of humans have been brought to think that humility means pretty women trying to believe they are ugly and clever men trying to believe they are fools. And since what they are trying to believe may, in some cases, be manifest nonsense, they cannot succeed in believing it, and we have the chance of keeping their minds endlessly revolving on themselves in an effort to achieve the impossible. (Emphasis added)

Screwtape's advice to Wormwood describes the situation which my friend found himself in when he misinterpreted Philippians 2:3. As I said earlier, my friend detected his mistake by noting how his mind was "endlessly revolving" on itself rather than being directed toward God and other people. We must think straight on this topic if we are to avoid such pitfalls. The scripture does not urge us to think about ourselves as negatively as possible, but to think as truthfully and as soberly as possible.

We can fail to view ourselves with "sober judgment" in two different ways. The word "sober" is especially appropriate, because both kinds of failure to view ourselves truthfully are noticeable in people who have had a bit too much to drink. First, there is the man whose self-opinion has been inflated by the alcohol. He thinks he is gallant, eloquent, courageous, and irresistibly attractive—and all the while he is behaving in a way that will make him blush at his folly the next morning. Secondly, there is the man whose intoxication makes him depressed. He is convinced he is wretched and useless, unloved and unlovable; he may also see himself as one unjustly abused and rejected by the world. Hero or monster, the drunken man's opinion of himself is false. Alcohol has turned his view of himself into a caricature of reality.

We can see these same two tendencies in people who have lost sober judgment or clear-mindedness through a psychological breakdown. I have talked to gifted, lovable, but severely depressed people who refused to believe that had any value as human beings. I have also talked to badly disturbed individuals who were convinced they were prophets, kings, or messiahs. An emotional breakdown has robbed both sets of people of the capacity to view themselves in an accurate and realistic way.

In fact, the Greek word Paul uses in Romans 12 that is translated as "sober judgment" can mean the opposite of madness. In Acts 26, Paul stands before King Agrippa, the King's wife Bernice, and the Roman procurator Porcius Festus to make his defense against the charges leveled against him by the Jewish leaders. After Paul testifies to his Damascus Road vision of the risen Lord and proclaims that Christ perfectly fulfills the Hebrew scriptures in his death and resurrection, Festus cries out, "Paul, you are mad; your great learning is turning you mad." (v.24). Festus, a sober-minded Roman official, views Paul's message about a resurrected Jewish messiah as wild nonsense. Paul responds by saying, "I am not mad, most excellent Festus, but I am speaking the sober truth." The Greek word for "sober" here is the same as in Romans 12:3. Paul's message is not unreal, a mere figment of a deluded imagination. Paul is sober, clear-headed, right-minded, and his proclamation is the accurate and sober truth.

Therefore, Paul's instruction in Romans 12:3 means that we should look at ourselves with good judgment, making a clear and accurate assessment of where we stand. We should neither view ourselves too highly or too lowly. The goal is clear thinking, not, as C.S. Lewis rightly says, "dishonesty" and "make-believe."

What Is the Truth About Ourselves?

We can now turn to an important question: What is the truth about ourselves? Many insecure and anxious people think they are the lowest of the low, unloved by others or by God. Other people are puffed up by pride; they think they are capable of any great accomplishment. However, neither the self-condemning nor the prideful know the truth.

There are two sets of basic truths about who we are that apply to every Christian man and woman. These truths should form our self-image. One set will help us avoid the pitfall of having too high a view of ourselves, and the other set will help us avoid having too low an opinion.

Truths That Keep Us in Our Place

A few minutes of serious meditation on God, the universe, and the human condition is a sure antidote for an inflated view of ourselves. God is awesome, holy, the sovereign creator of the universe. We are human beings—limited, finite, mortal, and dependent on a beneficent creation and creator. The contrast could hardly be more striking. The prophet Isaiah knew this truth well:

> Who has measured the waters in the hollow of his hand

> and marked off the heavens with a span,
> enclosed the dust of the earth in a measure
> and weighed the mountains in scales
> and the hills in a balance?
>
> Who has directed the Spirit of the Lord,
> > or as his counselor has instructed him?
>
> Whom did he consult for his enlightenment,
> > and who taught him the path of justice,
> > and taught him knowledge,
> > and showed him the way of understanding?
>
> Behold, the nations are like a drop from a bucket,
> > and are accounted as the dust on the scales;
> > behold, he takes up the isles like fine dust.
>
> Lebanon would not suffice for fuel,
> > nor are its beasts enough for a burnt offering.
>
> All the nations are as nothing before him,
> > they are accounted by him as less than nothing and emptiness.
>
> (Is 40:12-17)

There is nothing like the knowledge of the majestic, holy, and all-powerful God for putting human beings in their proper place.

The most important truths for bringing our opinion of ourselves down to earth revolve around our necessary dependence on God. The greatest temptation for the person with an inflated self-image is the temptation to self-sufficiency and independence. Unfortunately, much of the modern advice for people with low self-esteem leads us into this very temptation. We are urged to bolster our shaky egos, assert our true personalities, realize our full potential. In some circumstances, this advice might have value. However, it is dangerous when it is offered apart from an understanding of our total dependence on God. Anyone who thinks that his talents, strength, wisdom, and goodness are sufficient apart from God's help has far too high an opinion of himself. To think about ourselves with "sober judgment" means to recognize our need to submit our lives to God and rely upon him in everything. As Paul writes in 1 Corinthians 1:30-31: "He is the source of your life in Christ Jesus, whom God made our wisdom, our righteousness and sanctification and redemption; therefore, as it is written, 'Let him who boasts, boast of the Lord.'"

Any truly realistic and sober assessment of our lives must make us realize that Paul's words are indisputably true: We can boast of nothing except Christ Jesus. As a pastor in a Christian community, I have many opportunities to realize that only the Lord can give grace and wisdom, that only he can give salvation. People often bring problems to me that seem insoluble from a human point of view. Yet I often see the Lord step in and directly make a change. These experiences of God's direct intervention have impressed upon me a crucial truth: Only God's resources of wisdom and power can genuinely change lives. He can use us as his instruments, but what we usually view as our own resources are actually gifts from him. They are only packaged differently than the more direct and dramatic displays of divine power. Everything that seems to belong to us is in fact a gift from God. As Paul writes in 1 Corinthians 4:7: "What have you that you did not receive? If then you received it, why do you boast as if it were not a gift?" Therefore, "Let him who boasts, boast of the Lord."

Truths That Raise Us Up

Sober judgment also steers us away from the other extreme: the view that we are worthless. If megalomania and pride have no basis in reality, neither does self-pity.

The most important truth for giving us a proper level of self-respect and self-worth is the truth that God values us. God "chose us in him [Christ] before the foundation of the world, that we should be holy and blameless before him" (Eph 1:4). He created us in his own image and likeness, and gave us dominion over his creation as his appointed representatives (Gn 1:26; Ps 8). Though marred by sin, we are still valuable enough in his sight for him to purchase us "not with perishable things such as silver or gold, but with the precious blood of Christ" (1 Pt 1:18-19). God foreknew us in love, created us in love, and redeemed us in love—we are therefore very important to the most important being in the universe. We are immensely valuable, precious, to the monarch of all that is.

In the same section of *The Screwtape Letters* quoted earlier, C.S. Lewis (through the person of the demon Screwtape) points out both the greatness of God's love for the human race and how God wants humans to value themselves and others:

> To anticipate the Enemy's strategy, we must consider His aims. . . . He wants each man, in the long run, to be able to recognize all creatures (even himself) as glorious and excellent things. He wants to kill their animal self-love as soon as possible; but it is His long-term policy, I fear, to restore to them a new kind of self-love—a charity and gratitude for all selves, including their own. . . . For we must never forget what is the most repellent and inexplicable trait in our Enemy; He really loves the hairless bipeds He has created, and always gives back to them with His right hand what He has taken away with His left.

Screwtape is right. God's aim is to have us view all creatures, including ourselves, as "glorious and excellent things." We are to view ourselves in this way because this is the most basic truth of who we are as God's creatures.

It's not easy to keep these truths in balance. Christians sometimes speak about God's love and grace in a way that excessively diminishes our value as human beings. "How great is God's love. I'm wretched, worthless, and totally unlovable, yet God still loves me." There is a grain of truth here. As Paul reminds us in Romans 5:6-8, God demonstrates the greatness of his love most clearly by redeeming those who have rebelled against him: "But God shows his love for us in that while we were yet sinners Christ died for us." Nonetheless, this does not mean that we have no *intrinsic value* in God's sight. We have rebelled, and have not "merited" God's saving love. But we still have a special place before God as creatures created in his own image and likeness. Even in the midst of our sin we have a special dignity and value.

We are valuable to God, not because of what we have done, but because of who we are as his creatures. This value is only increased by our being fully a part of God's own people. The scripture is full of expressions which convey the worth that God's people have in his sight. Sometimes they are called "the apple of God's eye" (Ps 17:8; Zec 2:8). God cares for and values his people like the pupil of his own eye. Another significant expression is found in Exodus 19:5, where God says, "You shall be my own possession among all peoples." The Hebrew word for "possession" here could also be translated "special treasure." It refers to an article that is prized highly and guarded carefully. God values us as the apple of his eye, as a special treasure, because he has created us in his own image and likeness, and because he has redeemed us from sin and made us his own people.

Many Christians have trouble applying this truth personally. We often believe in God's love in a general and abstract way without applying this truth specifically and concretely to ourselves. Many of us find it much easier to say "God loves the human race, God loves his people" than to say "God loves and values *me*."

I gained some insight into this phenomenon through an experience a few years ago. While meditating on some spiritual topic, I was suddenly struck by the realization that God loved and valued *me*. He knew me personally and he was pleased that I was serving him. This truth had never hit me with such force. I had always thought of God's love for me in the light of God's gracious character and his love for all human beings. The idea that this loving God knew me and valued me *as an individual* and not only as part of a crowd had a significant impact on me. It built my confidence and my thankfulness to God.

A second truth that raises us up is the truth that each of us has gifts and abilities to be used to serve God and our brothers and sisters. We all have a contribution to make. Paul is very clear and insistent on this point: "To each is given the manifestation of the Spirit for the common good" (1 Cor 12:7). When we become part of God's people, each of us is given gifts of service and a role to play in the plan of God. None of us are useless. Each of us has gifts and strengths; each part of the body is needed if the whole body is to function with vitality and strength.

This is a truth that many Christians find difficult to believe. Often our tasks and responsibilities seem so slight and insignificant—especially in comparison with what we see others doing. "I'm tired of serving coffee, setting up chairs, looking after children, licking envelopes (or whatever). I want to do something important, something useful, something that makes a real contribution." Evidently this is not merely a modern problem, for the apostle Paul addresses it quite directly:

> For just as the body is one and has many members, and all the members of the body, though many, are one body, so it is with Christ. . . . If the foot should say, 'Because I am not a hand, I do not belong to the body,' that would not make it any less a part of the body. And if the ear should say, 'Because I am not an eye, I do not belong to the body,' that would not make it any less a part of the body. If the whole body were an eye, where would be the hearing? If the whole body were an ear, where would be the sense of smell? But as it is, God arranged the organs in the body, each one of them, as he chose. If all were a single organ, where would the body be? As it is, there are many parts, yet one body. The eye cannot say to the hand, "I have no need of you," nor again the head to the feet, "I have no need of you." On the contrary, the parts of the body which seem to be weaker are indispensable. . . . Now you are the body of Christ and individually members of it.
> (1 Cor 12:12, 14-22, 27)

According to Paul, each of us has an important gift to use in serving the body of Christ. Some gifts may appear more important than others, but in fact all of them are indispensable. The little humble gifts of love and service in Christ's body allow the body to fulfill its mission in the world, even more than the prominent and much envied gifts of preaching and teaching.

I have seen a perfect example of this spiritual

principle in the life of my own mother. My family is Jewish, and my mother came to know the Lord a few months after my conversion. At this time she was recovering from a serious heart attack, and was confined to her bedroom. As my mother grew in her relationship with the Lord, she began to experience a strong desire to serve him in some significant way. But how could she—a semi-invalid with little Christian training or experience—provide any significant service? She struggled with this dilemma daily, even after recovering some of her strength. What was she to do? The answer came to her one day as she was praying. "Of course! This is what I can do! I cannot preach, and I cannot minister to the sick, but I can certainly pray!" So pray she did. Daily she sought the Lord in worship and intercession. Her confidence and her contentment now began to grow. Gradually she started seeing other little things she could do in service—telephoning friends who needed encouragement, showing hospitality, serving her husband. She soon had more work on her hands than she could possibly do. She could not serve in a highly visible position, but she knew that her humble service pleased the Lord and contributed to the advancement of his kingdom.

We all have gifts, we all have strengths, we all have an important part to play in the work of God. This is a truth that we must believe and appropriate in our lives. If we are all needed to do the Lord's work, how can we be worthless?

Seeing Ourselves As God Sees Us

Viewing ourselves truthfully, with sober judgment, simply means seeing ourselves the way God sees us. Of course, to seek God's mind is the way a Christian learns the truth about anything. Finding out the truth about ourselves is no exception. God is the great expert on who and what we are, as the psalmist writes:

> O Lord, you have searched me and you know me.
> You know when I sit and when I rise;
>   you perceive my thoughts from afar.
> You discern my going out and my lying down;
>   you are familiar with all my ways.
> Before a word is on my tongue
>   you know it completely, O Lord.
>   (Ps 139:1-4)

God knows you far better than your spouse, parents, or close friends know you. He knows you far better than you know yourself. He sees every weakness, he notices every strength. He recognizes your limitations, he perceives your gifts. He knows every sinful act, but he also knows your righteousness, dedication, and love. When he looks at you, God sees the good and the bad—but, above all, he sees a creature created in his own image and likeness, originally destined for glory and perfection, now redeemed from bondage to sin and placed in the beloved Son who sits on his right hand in royal splendor.

This is how we should strive to see ourselves—accurately, truthfully, neither yielding to inflated visions nor to self-hatred and self-pity. In the apocryphal/deuterocanonical book of Sirach, the author puts it like this:

> My Son, be modest in your self-esteem,
> and value yourself at your proper worth.
> Who can justify a man who runs himself down,
> or respect a man who despises himself?
> (Sirach 10:28-29)

We should be "modest" in our self-esteem, and not "run ourselves down." This is how to look at ourselves with sober judgment.

THREE

Timidity

Before discussing the meaning of true Christian humility, I would like to examine a related emotional difficulty that often masquerades as humility—a difficulty with timidity. Once again, we find an emotional problem disguised as a Christian virtue.

Many people are timid. Often this problem is another manifestation of low self-worth and emotional insecurity. We fear that others will disapprove of us if we speak out, sing out, or make ourselves conspicuous. We fear that we will fail or make a mistake, and we fear that we will make a fool of ourselves. Some of us feel timid and self-conscious when others look at us for any length of time; we feel certain that they are thinking badly of us. Since we do not see ourselves as valuable or gifted, we believe that people who notice us will not like us or respect us. Thus, we avoid prominence and visibility because we lack confidence in who we are. At the root of such timidity one can usually find a problem with low self-worth.

God does not want his people bound by timidity and lack of self-confidence. Christians should be bold, confident, and decisive. True, we must be careful to avoid a wrong self-assertiveness or personal ambition, but a healthy Christian personality is not one that is dominated by shyness and timidity.

Timidity Disguised as Humility

A friend of mine in the Christian community I am a part of told me an illuminating story about himself. My friend was by temperament shy and reserved. When he attended large community meetings, he always arranged to sit in the back of the room in as inconspicuous a place as possible. He never spoke at these meetings. In smaller groups, he spoke quietly, gently, and with apparent reluctance.

His retiring demeanor did not go unnoticed. Eventually several people in the community came to him and told him how much they admired his humility. Of course, he found these words very encouraging. After all, he thought, humility is one of the most important Christian virtues. He was glad to know he was making progress in this aspect of his Christian life.

Then one day while praying, this man was surprised to experience the Lord trying to tell him something about his personality. The conviction began to grow within him that the Lord was actually angry with his "humility." He sensed the Lord saying something like this: "What you are calling 'humility' is in fact an emotional weakness that I've wanted to change in you for a long time. Repent of your shyness and timidity, and begin to serve your brothers and sisters."

"Serve your brothers and sisters"—timidity usually prevents us from doing this. What clearer indication do we need that timidity is not to be equated with humility? In fact, as we shall see later, the essence of humility involves taking on the mind of a servant. Since timidity prevents us from serving others, it is the direct opposite of humility.

Though I am not generally a fearful person, I have occasionally experienced a temptation to be timid in a way that would work against my serving others. One example of this is speaking up at Bible studies or prayer meetings when there is time for open sharing. Many times I've sat tensely glued to my chair, knowing that I had something to share that would be helpful to others present, but nevertheless afraid to stand up and speak. Most times I have conquered the fear and spoken out—and the fear always diminishes dramatically. But there have been times when timidity kept me from giving to others what God had given to me.

There are many other common situations in which timidity works against love and service. Evangelism is one example. How difficult it is at times to identify yourself as a Christian, to speak with someone directly about their need for God, to invite someone to go with you to a church service or to some other Christian event where they can encounter the Lord. Another example is reluctance to use special gifts, such as gifts of music. Timidity sometimes keeps us from using our voices or instrumental abilities to glorify the Lord and build up our brothers and sisters. Other examples from daily life abound. Some people fear making telephone calls, and therefore fail to convey important information or to encourage friends or build personal relationships. These examples are not uncommon; I have seen them operate in the lives of too many people. Far too often timidity prevents us from loving and serving those whom God has called us to love and serve.

If timidity so obviously inhibits our ability to serve others, how do we ever get away with disguising it as humility? The answer, as we shall discuss later in greater detail, is that timidity appears virtuous because it resembles a genuine aspect of Christian humility—freedom from self-assertion and the consuming human desire for publicity, position, status, and recognition. Our fear of putting ourselves forward and making ourselves visible can easily be interpreted (by others and by ourselves) as a virtuous contempt for worldly pomp and glory. Fortunately, this disguise is not so difficult to uncover. Timidity is an emotional bondage, a fear of position, status, of being seen and being known. True humility involves a choice not to make these things the goals in life. The humble person is free from the desire for high position, but the humble person is also able to receive status and position if these are part of God's purposes for him.

This brief look at timidity as an emotional problem should convince us that Satan will try to bind human beings with this fear. If he can keep us timid, he can hinder our efforts to love and serve others and at the same time make us unhappy. For after all, timidity is a very uncomfortable condition. It usually springs from doubts about self-worth, and it greatly contributes to insecurity, lack of confidence, and self-doubt. Therefore, Satan has won an important battle if he successfully holds us to patterns of timidity. If he can also manage to convince us that this bondage is in fact a Christian virtue which we should thank God for, he has, in the words of C.S. Lewis, introduced "an element of dishonesty and make-believe" in our Christian lives. This is a major deception, a product of the enemy's effective propaganda machine. Christians should not let themselves be tricked by this tactic, but should resist it with God's truth.

Walking in Boldness

The truth is that scripture nowhere speaks of timidity as a fruit of the Spirit. In fact, the exact opposite is the case. The scripture is full of exhortations to confidence and boldness, and it gives many examples of men and women of God who exhibited these qualities.

The classic text on timidity is found in 2 Timothy 1:6-8:

> Hence I remind you to rekindle the gift of God that is within you through the laying on of my hands; for God did not give us a spirit of timidity but a spirit of power and love and self-control. Do not be ashamed then of testifying to

our Lord, nor to me his prisoner, but share in suffering for the gospel in the power of God.

This passage can best be understood in the light of another related passage from 1 Timothy:

> Command and teach these things. Let no one despise your youth, but set the believers an example in speech and conduct, in love, in faith, in purity. . . . Do not neglect the gift you have, which was given you by prophetic utterance when the council of elders laid their hands upon you. (1 Tm 4:11-12, 14)

Timothy was a young man in his middle thirties when Paul wrote these letters to him. He had traveled and worked with Paul for about fifteen years, and was then installed over the church at Ephesus as Paul's representative. This put Timothy in a rather challenging position. He was supposed to rule authoritatively over a community of men and women, many of whom were older than himself (see 1 Tm 5:1-2, 4:12). Some people also infer from other passages (1 Cor 16:10-11, 1 Tm 5:23) that Timothy may have had a naturally timid and nervous temperament. Finally, as Paul's close associate, Timothy would naturally be compared with his formidable teacher. Thus, Timothy faced a difficult situation as head of the church at Ephesus.

Paul responds to the difficulties of Timothy's situation by exhorting him to stir up the gift he had received when he had been ordained for his ministry in Ephesus. Timothy is not to be timid or afraid. The Lord has clearly set him aside for the work he is doing, and he should pursue it with confidence, boldness, and courage. The Spirit he has received from God—the Holy Spirit—is not a spirit of timidity, but of "power and love and self-control." Paul does not sympathize with Timothy; instead, he urges him to lay aside timidity and walk in boldness.

There are many other examples in the scripture of men who overcome timidity in order to do the work that God gives them. One of the most vivid examples is Moses. When God first appears to Moses in the burning bush and commissions him to free the children of Israel from bondage in Egypt, Moses responds very cautiously. First, he questions whether God has really chosen the right man:

> But Moses said to God, "Who am I that I should go to Pharaoh, and bring the sons of Israel out of Egypt?" (Ex 3:11)

God reassures Moses that he is indeed the right man, and that God himself will go with him. Next Moses protests that the people of Israel will not believe what he has to say, much less Pharaoh and the Egyptians:

> Then Moses answered, "But behold, they will not believe me or listen to my voice, for they will say, 'The Lord did not appear to you.'"
> (Ex 4:1)

50 The Self-Image of a Christian

God patiently disposes of this objection by giving Moses some miraculous signs he can perform to authenticate his claims. Then Moses protests that he is not a very good speaker, and will probably fail to muster the eloquence that the deliverance will require.

> But Moses said to the Lord, "Oh, my Lord, I am not eloquent, either heretofore or since thou hast spoken to thy servant; but I am slow of speech and of tongue." (Ex 4:10)

This time the Lord responds a little more abruptly:

> Then the Lord said to him, "Who has made man's mouth? Who makes him dumb, or deaf, or seeing, or blind? Is it not I, the Lord? Now therefore go, and I will be with your mouth and teach you what you shall speak." (Ex 4:12)

Finally, Moses blurts out in desperation the words he has been thinking all along:

> But he said, "Oh, my Lord, send, I pray, some other person." (Ex 4:13)

The Lord is now a bit exasperated with Moses. He gives one concession—Aaron will do the speaking—but as for the rest, Moses is the man for the job, and he is not going to wriggle free:

> Then the anger of the Lord was kindled against Moses and he said, "Is there not Aaron, your

brother, the Levite? I know he can speak well. . . . And you shall speak to him and put the words in his mouth" (Ex 4:14a, 15a)

Moses demonstrates a great deal of boldness (what the Jews call "chutzpah") in his bargaining with God. However, this boldness is only inspired by his terror of returning to Egypt. At this point, his fear of Egypt exceeds his fear of God.

Moses does not handle himself like a heroic champion. In this first encounter with the God of Abraham, Isaac, and Jacob, he shows much ingenuity, but little courage. The following chapters of Exodus present a very different picture. Moses marches repeatedly to the throne of one of the most powerful monarchs in the world demanding that the people of Israel be allowed to go out to the wilderness and sacrifice to their God. The mighty Pharaoh resists strongly, but finally must yield to the boldness and power of this man who comes speaking in the name of the Lord. Moses successfully delivers the people of Israel from bondage in Egypt. Then he is confronted with an even more formidable task—governing the people whom he delivered. Time and time again Moses faces challenges from other nations, challenges from his own hungry and disgruntled people, challenges from ambitious young men who resent his leadership, and even challenges from members of his own family. And time and time again Moses responds with firmness and decisiveness, without a hint of timidity. Surely we see here a changed man.

Another example of God's power overcoming the timidity of his servants is Jeremiah. God's first reported encounter with Jeremiah reminds us both of Timothy and Moses:

> Now the word of the Lord came to me saying,
> "Before I formed you in the womb I knew
>   you,
>   and before you were born I consecrated
>   you;
>   I appointed you a prophet to the nations."
> Then I said, "Ah, Lord God! Behold I do not
>   know how to speak, for I am only a youth."
> But the Lord said to me,
>   "Do not say, 'I am only a youth';
>   for to all to whom I send you you shall go,
>   and whatever I command you you shall
>   speak.
>   Be not afraid of them, for I am with you to
>   deliver you, says the Lord."

Jeremiah was young and lacked confidence that he could properly represent the Lord. The Lord reassures Jeremiah that he is indeed the right man for the job, just as he reassured Moses, and just as Paul later reassures Timothy. Timidity is a common response to God's call in the scripture, but God refuses to accept it as an excuse for laying aside the yoke of his service.

We could point to many other examples of the boldness and confidence of God's servants: John the Baptist denouncing sin, Jesus cleansing the temple, Peter and the Twelve standing before the

Sanhedrin, the apostle Paul confuting his opponents and proclaiming the gospel. These were humble men, but also men of great boldness. Humility and boldness can and should go together. Humility should not be confused with timidity, any more than with having a low opinion of ourselves. With these points in mind we are ready to examine the real nature of Christian humility.

FOUR

True Humility: The Mind of a Servant

The most important passage on humility in the New Testament is the one from which my friend drew his unsuccessful humility-drills: Philippians 1:27-2:11.

> Only let your manner of life be worthy of the gospel of Christ, so that whether I come and see you or am absent, I may hear of you that you stand firm in one spirit, with one mind striving side by side for the faith of the gospel, and not frightened in anything by your opponents. This is a clear omen to them of their destruction, but of your salvation, and that from God. For it has been granted to you that for the sake of Christ you should not only believe in him but also suffer for his sake, engaged in the same conflict which you saw and now hear to be mine.
>
> So if there is any encouragement in Christ, any incentive of love, any participation in the Spirit, any affection and sympathy, complete my joy by being of the same mind, being in full accord and of one mind. Do nothing from selfishness or conceit, but in humility count others

better than yourselves. Let each of you look not only to his own interests, but also to the interests of others. Have this mind among yourselves, which is yours in Christ Jesus, who, though he was in the form of God, did not count equality with God a thing to be grasped, but emptied himself, taking the form of a servant, being born in the likeness of men. And being found in human form he humbled himself and became obedient unto death, even death on a cross. Therefore God has highly exalted him and bestowed on him the name which is above every name, that at the name of Jesus every knee should bow, in heaven and on earth and under the earth, and every tongue confess that Jesus Christ is Lord, to the glory of God the Father.

This is surely the richest and weightiest teaching on Christian humility found in all of scripture. Therefore, we will devote the next two chapters to a study of this passage with the hope of capturing the true meaning of Christian humility.

"In Full Accord And of One Mind" (Phil 1:27-2:2)

The first striking fact about this passage is the context of the teaching on humility: Paul strongly links humility with an exhortation to love and unity. Paul begins this passage by packing into a few sentences a host of images having to do with unity: "stand firm in one spirit, with one mind striving side by side for the faith of the gospel," "complete my joy by being of the same mind, being in full accord and of one mind." The phrase "participation in the Spirit" literally means "fellowship in the Spirit" or "community in the Spirit." The word for "participation" in Greek is *koinonia*; it either refers to the unity the church has *with* the Spirit of God or with one another *in* the Spirit of God. Paul obviously has a deep concern that the church in Philippi be united as one body.

The reason for this emphasis on unity is clear from the context. If the Philippian church is to witness powerfully to the gospel, it must manifest the oneness among brothers and sisters that life in Christ brings: "Only let your manner of life be worthy of the gospel of Christ. . . . with one mind striving side by side for the faith of the gospel. . . ." Truly effective Christian service requires a truly united Christian people. This is especially the case when there is great opposition to the gospel, as there was in Philippi: ". . . not frightened in anything by your opponents;" "for it has been granted to you that for the sake of Christ you should . . . also suffer for his sake, engaged in the same conflict which you saw and now hear to be mine." Paul knows what it means to face conflict in the service of the gospel—he writes this letter from prison, probably in Ephesus, and his first stay in Philippi also involved some stormy confrontations that resulted in a short prison term (Acts 16). He knows from personal experience the importance of not fighting the battle alone, but instead "striving side by side" with brothers and sisters in Christ "for the faith of the gospel."

The unity Paul urges on the Philippians is a unity built upon committed Christian love—*agape*. This is evident from verses 1-2:

> So if there is any encouragement in Christ, any incentive of love, any participation in the Spirit, any affection and sympathy, complete my joy by being of the same mind, having the same love, being in full accord and of one mind.

The Christian people are not just a randomly assembled body of individuals united by a common goal and a common opposition; they are a new family held together by bonds of brotherly love and fidelity. It is the love inspired by sharing the same inheritance "in Christ" and "in the Spirit" that allows the Christian people to enjoy true unity.

But how is this unity to be lived out in daily life? What traits of character and practical principles of conduct are required if this oneness in love is to be achieved? Now we come to the heart of Paul's message in Philippians 2: The key to unity in love is Christian humility.

"In Humility Count Others Better Than Yourselves" (Phil 2:3-4)

In verses 3-4, Paul proceeds to give some basic but important instructions on humility:

> Do nothing from selfishness or conceit, but in humility count others better than yourselves.

Let each of you look not only to his own interests, but also to the interests of others.

This passage includes the teaching discussed at the very beginning of this book: "count others better than yourselves." My zealous friend took this to mean that he should compare himself with others and consider them "better$—that is, as more valuable or talented or virtuous than he. A few weeks effort at implementing this teaching convinced my friend that he had misunderstood the passage. The wise comment of C.S. Lewis applies perfectly to this misinterpretation of Philippians 2:3: "By this method thousands of humans have been brought to think that humility means pretty women trying to believe they are ugly and clever men trying to believe they are fools."

The understanding or misunderstanding of these verses hinges on the word "better." In the common usage of today, my friend made the most reasonable interpretation possible by taking "better" to mean "superior in value, ability, or virtue." However, in many societies of the past this word (and other words like it such as "superior" and "inferior") had a different meaning. It referred to social position and the master-servant relationship. One could imagine English house servants of a century ago admonishing their children with the words, "Mr. and Mrs. Russell are your betters, so you must show them greater respect." One's "betters" were those "over" one in the accepted structure of society, those whom one was obliged to specially serve and honor.

An amusing example of this use of "betters" is found in J.R.R. Tolkien's trilogy, *The Lord of the Rings*. In the first book we meet old Ham Gamgee who for years has served as gardener for one of the wealthiest citizens of the Shire, Mr. Bilbo Baggins. Ham's son, Sam, has grown up practically at Mr. Bilbo's feet. There Sam has heard tales of dragons, dwarves, elves, mountains, and distant kingdoms. This causes his father some concern, and he advises his son in the following words: "Elves and dragons! . . . Cabbages and potatoes are better for me and you. Don't go getting mixed up in the business of your betters, or you'll land in trouble too big for you." The Gamgees relate to the Baggins' family as their betters—they serve them. As the plot develops, Sam becomes the personal servant of Frodo Baggins, Bilbo's heir, and travels loyally by his side through many dangers and adventures.

The command "Count others better than yourselves" could thus be accurately restated as, "Be a servant to others." The servant regards himself as one responsible to care for the needs and interests of those over him. He is at the disposal of others. He is not able to order his life according to his own preferences, but must subordinate his life and his ambitions to the needs and concerns of those he is serving. For us to regard others as "better" than ourselves means that we count others as people we are obligated to honor and serve and attend to.

This understanding of Philippians 2:3 is supported by the etymology of the Greek word for "humility." The word in Greek is literally "lowly-mindedness" (the RSV sometimes renders it "lowliness" as in Ephesians 4:2 and sometimes "humility"). The words "low" and "high" are used in many languages, including Hebrew and Greek, to designate social position. Kings, nobles, generals, and local governors held the highest positions, while servants and slaves held the lowest positions (unless they served a king, noble, general, or governor, in which case their position might be higher than many freedmen). To be "high-minded" thus means to act in an arrogant, haughty, and self-important manner, as though one were "over" others. To be "lowly-minded" means to be respectful, courteous, and at the disposal of others, as though one were a servant. Therefore, the very word for "humility" in Greek means taking on the mind of a servant.

The truly humble man is thus one who is willing to take the lowest position, the position of a servant. This can also be seen in another passage in scripture, Luke 14:7-11:

> Now he told a parable to those who were invited, when he marked how they chose the places of honor, saying to them, "When you are invited by any one to a marriage feast, do not sit down in a place of honor, lest a more eminent man than you be invited by him; and he who invited you both will come and say to you, 'Give your place to this man,' and then you will begin with shame to take the lowest place. But when you are invited, go and sit in the lowest place, so that when your host comes he may say to

you, 'Friend, go up higher;' then you will be honored in the presence of all who sit at table with you. For every one who exalts himself will be humbled, and he who humbles himself will be exalted."

The saying, "He who exalts himself [lifts himself up] will be humbled [lowered], and he who humbles himself will be exalted," is used by Jesus in other contexts as well (for example, Luke 18:14). It is an important truth aptly illustrated in Jesus' parable: The man who humbles himself by taking the lowest position is literally exalted to the head of the table. The humble man takes the lowest position, the position of the servant.

Therefore, humility does not mean evaluating others as superior in gifts or holiness or value; nor does it mean having a low opinion of oneself; nor does it mean acting timid, reserved, or afraid. Humility means taking on the mind of a servant, placing oneself at others' disposal. It means that "each of you look not to his own interests, but also to the interests of others."

"Do Nothing From Selfishness" (Phil 2:3)

Philippians 2:3 begins with the command, "Do nothing from selfishness or conceit." The two words, "selfishness" and "conceit," represent the great enemies and opposites of humility. In fact, the command to "do nothing from selfishness or conceit" is just another way of saying "be humble." Therefore, a look at each of these words should help us to understand more clearly what Christian humility is and what it is not.

The Greek word for "selfishness" (*eritheia*) could also be translated as "self-seeking" or "selfish ambition." In his book *New Testament Words*, William Barclay describes the origin and development of the word in secular Greek usage as follows:

> *Eritheia* therefore began by being a perfectly respectable word with the meaning 'labor for wages.' It then begins to degenerate. It began to mean that kind of work which is done for motives of pay and for nothing else; that kind of work which has no motive of service whatever and which has only one question—What do I get out of it? It therefore went on to mean 'canvassing and intriguing for public office.' It was the characteristic of the man who sought public office, not for any service he could render the State, but simply and solely for his own honour and glory and for his own profit. It then acquired two other meanings. First, it came to be used of 'party squabbles,' of the jockeying for position and the intriguing for place and power which is so often characteristic of both secular and ecclesiastical politics. Second, it ended up by meaning 'selfish ambition,' the ambition which has no conception of service and whose only aims are profit and power.

Eritheia thus means "self-seeking" in the sense of looking to further one's own interests at the expense of another's; it also means "selfish ambition" in the sense of seeking position and power. The "selfish" man is out to advance himself and his own position without regard to the needs or interests of others. He is the opposite of a servant.

This type of "self-seeking" or "selfish ambition" is often regarded in our society as a virtue rather than a vice. It finds a home in most of the professions—politics, business, education. In my time at the university, I was shocked to find the faculty members in my department divided into warring factions, each member seeking to advance his own career and policies. The pressure to succeed and move up the ladder in most large business corporations is also notorious. Few businesses attempt to foster in their employees a strong personal concern for their families and their co-workers— the incentives are more in the direction of advancing one's own position and career. In fact, a new word—"careerism"—has sometimes been used to describe the trend among many modern Americans to invest themselves totally in their personal advancement.

Selfish ambition can also be a serious temptation in more directly spiritual matters. For example, it is common for people in Christian organizations to battle with the "move-up-the-ladder" syndrome. This is the tendency to regard positions of responsibility and authority as rewards for good work that should be aggressively pursued rather than as roles in the body of Christ assigned by God. Another example of selfish ambition in the directly spiritual realm is "spiritual careerism." This refers to an intense preoccupation with one's future and one's "ministry." Some people can get so wrapped up with discerning and developing their gift as a teacher, preacher, evangelist, prophet, or healer that they neglect their more basic duty of serving the immediate needs of their brothers and sisters.

A more subtle form of spiritual careerism can be seen when a desire for perfect personal holiness collides with a call to service. Some Christians refuse to perform a service that will draw attention and respect from others because they "want to remain humble." For the purpose of maintaining a false "humility," Christians thus sometimes fail to heed God's call to serve others—the very meaning of true humility. This attitude amounts to putting one's own spiritual career and condition ahead of serving other people, advancing one's own spiritual welfare rather than looking "to the interests of others." Therefore, this is not true Christian humility but its opposite: spiritual self-seeking and selfish ambition.

There is an important truth to be drawn from this: Selfishness (*eritheia*) means striving for position and power with personal aggrandizement as a primary motive. It does not refer simply to holding positions of power nor to seeking after such positions. It is possible to seek after a position with the intention and goal of providing service. In some cases this is probably the humble thing to do. The critical issue concerns the intention and goal of the "ambition" and the manner in which it is pursued.

"Do Nothing From . . . Conceit" (Phil 2:3)

The second great enemy and opposite of humility presented in Philippians 2:3 is "conceit." The Greek word for "conceit" could be translated more literally as "empty glory" (the King James Bible uses the somewhat archaic English word "vainglory," with "vain" meaning "empty"). To do something from "empty glory" means to act out of a desire for your reputation, to act so that others will admire you, honor you, pay attention to you. This word is thus closely connected in meaning to "selfish ambition"—seeking a position where people will honor you. Like "selfish ambition," "conceit" does not characterize the true Christian servant, who freely takes the lowest and most inconspicuous place.

I had an experience several years ago which both revealed my own latent desire for "empty glory" and also confirmed its true "emptiness." I was invited to help organize and lead a national conference for Christian university students. My role required that I sit on the stage, deliver a key address, and preside at a general session. The prominence I would have at the conference excited me—it seemed to begin the fulfillment of my secret desires for fame and glory which I had tried to extinguish but which were still rumbling beneath the surface. The conference came, and my role was just as prominent as expected. Everyone knew who I was; people greeted me in the corridors with admiring glances. Yet the effect on me personally was the opposite of what I expected.

The attention quickly became burdensome rather than exciting. I wanted to leave the stage and hide in the last row of the auditorium. I then realized that all the recognition, attention, and honor that could be paid to me during that weekend were empty—not insincere or false, but unable to satisfy what I really wanted. My true desire was for the glory of God and his commendation. This realization early in the weekend freed me from thinking about myself and allowed me to approach the conference as a servant.

In order to understand what the scripture means by "empty glory," one must understand the broader scriptural teaching on "glory." Scripture does not teach that glory in itself is bad nor does it teach that we should never seek it. Instead, scripture offers us three important truths about glory. First, we should seek the true glory which comes from God rather than the empty glory which comes from men. God desires to give us his glory (Ps 84:11; 1 Thes 2:12; 1 Pt 5:4, 10; 2 Pt 1:3) and desires that we seek it (Rom 2:6-10). Seeking glory from men only interferes with seeking glory from God (Jn 5:44; Prv 25:27 in NAS). Second, scripture teaches that on certain occasions it is appropriate to receive honor from men. Many passages of scripture command us to honor various categories of people. We are to honor parents (Ex 20:12; Dt 5:16), leaders of the Christian community (1 Tm 5:17), masters (1 Tm 6:1), wives (1 Pt 3:7), widows (1 Tm 5:3), kings (1 Pt 2:17), Christians (Ps 15:4; Rom 12:10), and all men (1 Pt 2:7). Since all of us fall under at least one of these categories, all of us should at times receive special honor. We are not commanded to avoid receiving honor from men, but we are commanded to not seek after it. Third, scripture says that the key to receiving true honor and glory, the honor and glory that come from God, is humility. "A man's pride will bring him low, but he who is lowly in spirit will obtain honor" (Prv 29:23, see also Prv 15:33; 18:12; 22:4). As Jesus says, "Every one who exalts himself will be humbled, and he who humbles himself will be exalted" (Lk 14:11; 18:14). One must avoid seeking after "empty glory" if one wants to possess the true glory.

I have learned from experience that the desire for empty glory can spring from two very different sources. The first source is pride and ambition. When this is the case, the Christian solution is repentance. One should simply decide to change. The second source of the desire for empty glory is insecurity and feelings of low self-worth. The search for approval and recognition may be more of an attempt at self-reassurance than an act of proud self-exaltation. If this is the case, the "conceit" is still wrong, but repenting for it will probably not change the problem. In fact, trying to repent of "conceit" might only increase the severity of the problem by increasing the underlying personal insecurity. The solution lies rather in growing more secure and confident. Some type of repentance may be in order, but it would be repentance for attitudes of self-contempt and not for "conceit" or "pride."

Conclusion

A careful reading of scripture reveals that humility is different from what many of us think it is. Scripture teaches that humility means servanthood. To be humble means to put the interests and needs of others before your own, and to put yourself at others' disposal as a servant. Humility should not be confused with either timidity or a negative self-evaluation. It is not an introspective mental or emotional state, but is instead an outward-looking mentality which leads a person to care for others. Indeed, serving others well requires boldness, aggressiveness, and an accurate self-assessment.

Though the humble person must avoid all selfish ambition and conceit, this should not lead to an avoidance of responsibility. The commitment to serve will sometimes place you in positions of prominence. This is not inconsistent with Christian humility. In fact, Jesus teaches that Christian leaders must excel in humility (Lk 22:24-27; Mt 20:24-28). The key to Christian humility is not powerlessness, but the resolution to not seek gain, power, position, or attention for yourself, and to seek instead the good of your brothers and sisters.

FIVE

Jesus, The Perfect Model of Humility

Our discussion of the basic biblical teaching on humility is complete except for one feature that is central to most New Testament instruction on living the Christian life: the example of Jesus Christ. Christian teaching on how to live is concrete and personal—we are to "walk in the same way in which he walked" (1 Jn 1:6). This is because Christianity is not mainly a doctrinal system or a moral code, but a living relationship with a personal God. If we want to understand the Christian approach to humility, we must look at the life of Jesus Christ.

"Taking the Form of a Servant" (Phil 2:5-11)

The passage which we have used as our key text on humility, Philippians 2, has still more to say on this subject. It continues its teaching by citing the example of Jesus in verses which many scholars think is an ancient Christian hymn:

Have this mind among yourselves, which is yours in Christ Jesus, who, though he was in

> the form of God, did not count equality with God a thing to be grasped, but emptied himself, taking the form of a servant, being born in the likeness of men. And being found in human form he humbled himself and became obedient unto death, even death on a cross. Therefore God has highly exalted him and bestowed on him the name which is above every name, that at the name of Jesus every knee should bow, in heaven and on earth and under the earth, and every tongue confess that Jesus Christ is Lord, to the glory of God the Father. (Phil 2:5-11)

Do you want to know what true humility is, and how it is obtained? Paul's formula is simple: Have the attitude that Jesus had, think the way that Jesus thought.

This hymn to the Son of God shows him in the three successive stages of his existence: preincarnate Son, incarnate Servant, and exalted Lord. As the preincarnate Son, he existed in "the form of God," occupying a special place of dignity and privilege above all the works of creation. This provides *the setting* for Jesus' great demonstration of humility. Refusing to cling to the privileges already given him or to grasp at the privileges awaiting him, he was "born in the likeness of men," walking upon earth as the incarnate Word of God. The incarnation and the humiliating "death on a cross" constitute *the act* of humility, greater than any other, in which he who "was in the form of God", "emptied himself, taking the form of a servant" and "humbled himself," be-

Jesus, The Perfect Model of Humility 73

coming "obedient unto death, even death on a cross." Finally, God responds to Jesus' act of humility by raising him from the dead, enthroning him at his right hand as the exalted Lord, giving him the title which qualifies him to rule officially over all creation, and commanding every creature under heaven to worship him even as they would worship the Almighty Father himself. This is *the consequence* of the Son of God's humility.

This description in Philippians 2 of the setting, act, and consequence of Jesus' humility is the perfect illustration of the teaching Paul has given in the previous verses. If the Son of God had been influenced by selfish ambition or a desire for empty glory, he would never have given up the full privileges he enjoyed in the Father's presence and taken on human flesh. But because he was obedient to his Father and was looking "not only to his own interests, but also to the interests of others," he was willing to become a man, live an obscure life for thirty or more years, be attacked and rejected by most of his own people, and suffer the most shameful of deaths—"even death on a cross." The one who sat gloriously in the heights was now driven down to the deepest depths. The exalted Master had now taken the role of the lowly Servant. The King, to whom all owed homage, was putting the concerns and welfare of his people ahead of his own. This is the perfect example of humility.

But the hymn does not end here. Next we see Jesus enthroned in glory. This illustrates the important biblical principle, "He who humbles himself shall be exalted" (Lk 14:11; 18:14; James 4:10; 1 Pt 5:6). As stated in the last chapter, there is nothing wrong with being exalted, as long as God is the one who does the exalting. The master at table called forward the man who took the lowest position. In similar fashion, God the Father responds to Jesus' act of perfect humility with an act of perfect exaltation: "Therefore God has highly exalted him." Jesus again enters the glory of his Father, bringing with him his resurrected body and the blood that atones for the sins of the world, and being "designated" by his Father "Son of God in power according to the Spirit of holiness" (Rom 1:4).

None of us can ever fully imitate the humility of Jesus Christ. None of us ever begin from a position as high as his, and none of us can ever duplicate his act of humiliation. Still, his humility should serve as the pattern and model for our own.

"For I Have Given You an Example" (Jn 13:1-17)

The thirteenth chapter of John's Gospel presents a picture of Jesus very similar to that found in Philippians 2. Again, Jesus is shown as the man whose perfect humility is to be imitated by his disciples. In this case, Jesus expresses his servanthood memorably and clearly by using a symbolic action—the washing of his disciples' feet.

"Now before the feast of the Passover, when Jesus knew that his hour had come to depart out of this world to the Father, having loved his own who were in the world, he loved them to the end" (v.1). This sets the stage for the scene which is to follow. The vivid example of humble service which Jesus will offer in the washing of his disciples' feet occurs in the context of his strong and committed love for them. Humble service is one of the most important expressions of love.

"And during supper, when the devil had already put it into the heart of Judas Iscariot, Simon's son, to betray him, Jesus, knowing that the Father had given all things into his hands, and that he had come from God and was going to God, rose from supper, laid aside his garments, and girded himself with a towel" (vv.2-4). As in Philippians 2, the passage begins by reminding us of Jesus' true position as the Son of God—he came from God, he was going to God, and all creation was placed under his authority by God. This reminder of the Son's glory makes the following symbolic action of humble service stand out in proper relief.

"Then he poured water into a basin, and began to wash the disciples' feet, and to wipe them with the towel with which he was girded." (v.5). Jesus now attends to each of the disciples in turn, serving them in a manner appropriate to a slave. The Master suddenly takes the role of a Servant.

"He came to Simon Peter; and Peter said to him, 'Lord, do you wash my feet?' Jesus answered him, 'What I am doing you do not know now, but afterward you will understand.' Peter said to him, 'You shall never wash my feet.' Jesus answered him, 'If I do not wash you, you have no part in me' (vv.6-8). The Jews of Jesus' time had a strong sense of propriety in customs of honor and respect. One could not lightly perform a task seen as inappropriate to one's position in life. Therefore, we should not be surprised that at least one of the disciples speaks out against Jesus' highly irregular behavior. Here is Jesus, the Master and Teacher, performing menial service for his disciples. This in itself was unheard of. But these disciples knew that theirs was no ordinary master; this was the promised Messianic King, the Son of God, the fulfillment of all Israel's prophecies and hopes. Nonetheless, he refuses to heed Peter's protest. Although this was an unusual action—perhaps *because* this was an unusual action—Jesus sees it as crucial to perform.

"When he had washed their feet, and taken his garments, and resumed his place, he said to them, 'Do you know what I have done to you? You call me Teacher and Lord; and you are right, for so I am. If I then, your Lord and Teacher, have washed your feet, you also ought to wash one another's feet. For I have given you an example, that you also should do as I have done to you. Truly, truly, I say to you, a servant is not greater than his master; nor is he who is sent greater than he who sent him. If you know these things, blessed are you if you do them'" (vv.12-16).

Here Jesus explains to the disciples at least one of the reasons why he has humbled himself and washed their feet. He intends to give them an example they can imitate in their relationships with one another. Later in this same chapter Jesus says, "A new commandment I give to you, that you love one another; even as I have loved you, that you also love one another. By this all men will know that you are my disciples, if you have love for one another" (vv.34-35). The love commanded by Jesus requires that his disciples serve each other humbly. If they want to know about this humble service-love, they need only examine the life of their master and imitate it. If they do this well, the whole world will know whose disciples they are.

Again, as in the second chapter of Philippians, Jesus in John's Gospel is the perfect model of humility. Here is a man free from selfish ambition and a desire for empty human glory. He is not attached to his position of special privilege, but he lowers himself in a way that shocks his disciples in order to teach them an important lesson. Here is a man who is concerned for others and not merely for himself. Jesus is the perfect pattern of humility, the true Servant of God.

Two final observations can help us to understand this passage from the thirteenth chapter of John. First, Jesus washed his disciples' feet to teach them a lesson. He did not ordinarily express his servanthood by performing menial tasks for his disciples. In fact, his relationship with his disciples probably resembled closely the customary master-disciple relationships of his day. He expected his disciples to respect, obey, and serve him. We can see this from the rest of the gospels, but we can also see this from John 13 itself: The disciples react to Jesus' behavior with shock because he had never done anything quite like this before. They had been with him for about three years, and he had often surprised them, but never had he related to them as a slave, washing their feet!

This is an important point to understand. We could easily read John 13 and conclude that the only way to serve humbly is to take a low position and perform menial tasks. Should I then resign my supervisory position at work and find employment as a janitor? Or should I keep my position as supervisor and just relate to my subordinates as if I were a janitor? These are not the lessons of the footwashing episode. Jesus performed this menial task to teach his disciples a lesson. However, his ordinary way of serving them was by teaching them, training them, and making them into new men. He finally served them by offering up his life upon the cross as a sacrifice of atonement.

This brings us to our second observation. There is a deeper teaching in the footwashing episode in addition to a simple lesson about humble service. Let us recall the opening words of John 13: "Now before the feast of the Passover, when Jesus knew that his hour had come to depart out of this world to the Father, having loved his own who were in the world, he loved them to the end." The footwashing occurs during the last meal Jesus took with his disciples before his crucifixion. At this meal he was especially concerned to teach his disciples about the meaning of his life and his death. From the other gospels we know that Jesus instituted the Eucharist at this meal as a way of teaching about his sacrificial death and giving his disciples a way of remembering it together. The act of footwashing should be seen in the same light. In a simple and vivid act, Jesus taught his disciples about the meaning of his life and his impending death: He was the perfect Servant of God foretold in the scriptures, humbling himself in the incarnation and further humbling himself in the crucifixion, all in order to glorify his Father and bring life to the world. As in Philippians 2, Jesus' life of service is clearly manifested and fully consummated in his becoming "obedient unto death, even death on a cross."

Jesus, Sober-Minded and Confident

As the perfect model of true humility, Jesus is the perfect example of one who does not practice false humility. Jesus never degraded himself, nor did he ever yield to fear and timidity. He was a man of great confidence and self-assurance, yet one who never went beyond the limits set him by his Father.

Certainly no one ever thought that Jesus suffered from an overly-low opinion of himself. In fact, many of the Jewish leaders apparently thought his self-regard was too great. We can see why when we look at what Jesus had to say about himself. The words of Jesus recorded in John's Gospel assert strongly his unique position before God and his unique role in the Father's plan. Jesus forthrightly reveals his true identity: "I am the bread of life" (Jn 6:35); "I am the light of the world" (Jn 8:12); "I am the good shepherd" (Jn 10:11); "I am the resurrection and the life" (Jn 11:25-26); "I am the way, the truth, and the life"

(Jn 14:6). An equally strong statement is found in Mt 11:27: "All things have been delivered to me by my Father; and no one knows the Son except the Father, and no one knows the Father except the Son and any one to whom the Son chooses to reveal him." These are the sayings which elicited C.S. Lewis's frequently quoted remark: "A man who was merely a man and said the sort of things Jesus said would not be a great moral teacher. He would either be a lunatic—on a level with the man who says he is a poached egg—or else he would be the Devil of Hell."

Jesus spoke as he did for two reasons. First, these statements are all true. Jesus was neither a lunatic nor a demon. He was exactly who he said he was—the Son of God, the eternal "I am" (Jn 8:58). He had an accurate and clear perception of his identity. Secondly, people needed to know who he was. Jesus did not speak about himself in order to brag, but in order to offer men and women the new life he had come to bring. That was his mission. Therefore, he boldly assumed the position and role that his Father had appointed for him, and did not pretend to be anything other than what he truly was.

At the same time, Jesus never exalted himself above the position his Father assigned him. He never claimed to be superior to the Father, nor did he claim to be able to act independently of his Father. "Truly, truly, I say to you, the Son can do nothing of his own accord, but only what he sees the Father doing" (Jn 5:19. Also see Jn 5:30, 7:16, 7:28, 8:28). "The Father is greater than I" (Jn 14:28).

Jesus neither entertained an overly-low nor an overly-high opinion of himself. In all things he viewed himself with sober and accurate judgment.

Similarly, Jesus never yielded to fear and timidity. He spoke with confidence, even in the midst of great opposition; he acted decisively and aggressively, as seen in his cleansing of the temple (Mt 21:12-13). He could also be silent when appropriate, as in his trial before the Sanhedrin (Mt 26:63). Though he experienced fear (Mt 26:36-46), he never allowed his conduct and decisions to be determined by it. He was a man of strength and confidence whose perfect humility never served as a cloak for shyness, timidity, or fear.

Jesus Christ did not have a trace of false humility. If we follow his example, we will learn the true humility of a lowly servant, putting the interests of others ahead of our own, free from selfishness and conceit, but not indulging in self-contempt or timidity.

SIX

Overcoming Problems Of Self-Image

We have seen how our failure to distinguish between true and false humility can allow emotional disorders to hide under the form of Christian virtue. What looks at first like genuine self-effacing humility may turn out instead to be insecurity or lack of confidence.

In the previous chapters we have attempted to strip away the disguise and reveal these disorders for what they really are—emotional problems that need to be overcome. However, the exposure of the problem only begins the struggle to overcome it. The disorder is now visible and no longer camouflaged, but we must still develop an effective strategy to gain full freedom.

Christians who suffer from problems of self-image should begin by deciding they are willing and ready to fight. These problems are clearly not a part of God's perfect plan for our lives. They cut off our faith, foster discouragement and hopelessness, insulate us from encouragement and correction, and lead to self-pity and self-preoccupation. They thus prevent us from relating freely to God and to our brothers and sisters. They keep us from being servants in true Christian humility. Therefore, those of us who suffer from such problems have a powerful incentive to do what is necessary to be free of them.

Our strategy for overcoming problems of self-image should rely on the following seven principles: (1) acknowledgement; (2) repentance; (3) truth; (4) encouragement; (5) humility; (6) patience; and (7) prayer. We will now examine each of these principles.

Acknowledgement

This first principle in dealing with low self-worth takes us back one step: We must candidly and clearly acknowledge the problem. This involves more than just a general and abstract understanding of the difference between true and false humility. We must personally recognize a disorder in ourselves that needs to be corrected.

The first step in overcoming any problem is to diagnose it accurately and to understand how it works. For example, a physician cannot effectively treat a physical ailment until he diagnoses its nature and understands its cause. Thus, medical science has invested tremendous sums of money in developing sophisticated diagnostic tests. The physician must know what kind of problem he is dealing with before he can effectively treat it. If he does not know the nature of the ailment, or if the patient refuses to believe his diagnosis, then little progress can be made.

Many people who suffer from some type of self-image problem neither diagnose their problem accurately nor accept the true diagnosis when they hear it. Many resemble a skeptical patient who stubbornly clings to the notion that his stomach ulcer is actually a pulled abdominal muscle. The main reason for such resistance is that people with low self-worth usually accept the image of themselves provided by their emotional difficulty. When they are told that they have a problem with self-worth, they respond like this: "Oh no, I don't have a problem with how I look at myself. Sure, sometimes I get down on myself, but that's understandable; my real problem is that I'm a good-for-nothing who nobody loves," or "My real problem is that I'm not as talented or handsome as other people," or "My real problem is that life has given me a raw deal." The lie is swallowed, digested, and totally assimilated. These people cannot believe that the problem is not with themselves, but with how they see themselves.

As long as we trust fully in our own subjective experience of who we are and discount God's revelation and the evaluation of our brothers and sisters, we will not be able to change and grow stronger as men and women of God. The first step in overcoming a problem with a negative self-image is to face the problem squarely: Our view of ourself is not based on hard objective reality, but on an emotional weakness that needs to change.

Repentance

As we saw earlier, a person with low self-esteem should not earnestly repent for the "pride" or "conceit" which is in fact only a manifestation of his or her problem. This type of repentance misses the real source of the behavior and only aggravates the underlying insecurity. However, a person suffering from low self-esteem should repent in a way that focuses his or her will on the important underlying problems that need to change.

Before looking at these underlying problems, we need to clarify the meaning of true repentance. Sometimes we can think of repentance as referring mainly to an emotion—remorse or sorrow for sin. Remorse is certainly part of repentance, but it is not the most important part. Repentance mainly consists of an act of the will, and involves renunciation of sin, an act of *turning aside*. Therefore, when we repent for something, we do not merely feel bad about it; we also resolve to not do it again.

People with low self-esteem should repent seriously for failures in two main areas. First, we should repent for believing lies about ourselves. Most of us who have a problem with low self-esteem have developed an entrenched habit of listening submissively to the lies about ourselves which are continually aired in our minds. It's as though we are plugged into a round-the-clock radio broadcast pumping us full of enemy propaganda. Twelve o'clock show: "You really don't have any valuable gifts or abilities." Three o'clock: "No one really likes or respects you very much." And the special nightly news summary: "You can't do anything right! As usual, you mishandled every situation you encountered today. What's the use?" As we gullibly receive these distortions, insinuations, and outright fabrications, our negative view of ourselves deepens and expands.

If we have already acknowledged squarely that we have a problem with our self-image (our first principle), we should be able to acknowledge that these daily broadcasts greatly distort the truth. They reflect our problem rather than an accurate and sober picture of reality. Now we need to exercise our will in resisting these false assertions and in repenting when we fail to resist. We must repent for our gullibility, grow in wisdom to discern the true from the false, and steadfastly resist all seductive lies.

Secondly, we need to repent for yielding to the self-pity or self-preoccupation that usually follows an extended period of listening to our "negative self-image" radio station. Once we are convinced of our worthlessness, we withdraw from those around us and begin to think mainly about ourselves. How did I come to be this way? Why do I have to bear this burden? How can I get people to love me? Questions such as these lead us into a psychological maze that plunges us deeper and deeper into ourselves, until we totally lose our grip on the truth. The people around us find us moody, depressed, introspective, and unable to serve with eagerness and joy.

If we have successfully repented of believing lies about ourselves, we will have few occasions to repent of acting on the basis of these lies. However, total success will probably not come immediately, and we may well have occasion to repent also of self-pity and introspection. Moreover, for some of us, self-pity and introspection have become such habitual tenants that they will have to be forcibly evicted; they will not leave peacefully just because we no longer listen to lies about ourselves. Therefore, we must be ready to resist both the lies about ourselves and the temptations to self-pity and self-preoccupation that often follow them. We should eagerly repent each time we fail to resist these temptations.

Truth

Repentance means change: a turning away from lies and a turning toward the truth, a turning away from self-centeredness and a turning toward humility. The positive change demanded by the first act of repentance is the full appropriation of the truth about ourselves. It is not enough to simply turn off the station that broadcasts enemy propaganda; we must also turn on the station that broadcasts God's truth. We need to understand his truth thoroughly, and then lay hold of it with certainty and conviction.

In Chapter Two we discussed the basic truths which should form the way we look at ourselves. Two of these truths especially apply to people who have a problem with low self-esteem. First, God created each of us in his own image and likeness. He created us with worth and value, and he ransomed us back to himself at the cost of his Son's life. He loves us all, not only as a people, but also as particular individuals. Therefore, our position before God is one of tremendous dignity, and it is

Overcoming Problems of Self-Image 89

cause for considerable self-respect.

Secondly, God has given each of us gifts and abilities that we should use to serve him and to serve one another. None of us lacks the ability to contribute substantially to the Lord's work and to his people. Though our gifts differ in degree of visibility, they are all indispensable in the Lord's plan. Therefore, we should humbly and gratefully use the gifts that God has given us, and not esteem them more lightly than God does.

These are fundamental truths which apply to all of us. In addition, we should understand and lay hold of certain specific truths about ourselves. It is helpful to know where our gifts and strengths lie. It is helpful to know how other people value us. The best way to learn and appropriate these truths about ourselves is through the evaluation of other people, especially our brothers and sisters in the Lord. We should seek the evaluation of others, especially those whose judgment and wisdom we respect.

Many of us have a tendency to dismiss the positive evaluation that others give us. We spontaneously welcome their words with the thought, "they're just trying to be nice." This attitude is inappropriate. We should be suspicious of our own subjective judgment about ourselves for it often reflects a problem with low self-esteem.

Indeed, it is often the case that other people can make a better objective assessment of our gifts and strengths than we can. Several years ago, I had a conversation with an older Christian man that clearly illustrates this point. I had been serving for a short time in a minor pastoral position under the direct supervision of this man. I had never seriously considered doing any major pastoral work. In fact, I did not think that I was especially good at it. One day, as my friend and I were discussing my current responsibilities, he shocked me by saying, "You know, Mark, I think you have very strong pastoral gifts. You should consider devoting your life to this type of work." Immediately after the shock came disbelief. Although I respected this man highly and had great trust in his judgment, his perception of my pastoral abilities differed drastically from my own. Nevertheless, I decided to act on his judgment. I continued to do pastoral work and waited to see how our differing views stood up over time. The years that followed seemed to confirm his view rather than my own. This incident has made me much more cautious in accepting my own assessment of my gifts and strengths, especially when it conflicts with the assessment of others.

In short, to overcome problems with low self-worth, we must absorb the truth about ourselves. As in so many other areas of the Christian life, laying hold of the truth with faith is of primary importance. As Jesus said in a very different context, "You will know the truth, and the truth will make you free" (John 8:32).

Encouragement

The fourth principle for overcoming problems with self-image is the principle of encouragement:

Overcoming Problems of Self-Image

We should receive encouragement from our brothers and sisters in the Lord. This point is closely connected to the previous discussion about receiving the evaluation of others. However, the principle of encouragement is broader. It means that we should receive affection, love, respect, and personal support, as well as evaluation.

Human beings develop their self-image in the context of a set of personal relationships. A poor self-image often results from inadequacies in a person's important relationships early in life. Therefore, one would expect that strong, supportive relationships in the present could help compensate for some of the less supportive relationships of the past. Experience seems to confirm this hypothesis. The affection and encouragement that come from loyal, committed relationships can have great strengthening and healing power.

When I was a student at The University of Michigan, I had the chance to live for several months with a group of young Christian men who had a house near campus. I had never lived among a group of committed Christians before, and I did not know what to expect. The household had a number of customs that especially struck me. At the end of each meal we would all greet one another, one by one, and express our respect and affection for one another. At the end of each day we would gather in the living room and tell one another about the things we experienced during the day, both good and bad. If one brother had had a hard day, others would encourage him or give him helpful advice. Soon I found myself speaking personally to these men about things in my life that I had never revealed to anyone before, not even to my closest friends. The atmosphere of mutual love, respect, deep commitment, and loyalty filled the household; it evoked trust, and instilled strength and confidence. After living with these men for four months, I realized that I had been permanently changed for the better—strengthened, encouraged, and inspired with greater confidence. This is the power found in loyal, committed relationships.

In practical terms, this principle of encouragement has two main implications. First, we should do what we can to participate in a set of supportive relationships. For Christians, this means finding the right place in the body of Christ. We should actively pursue relationships in our church, fellowship, community, prayer group, or outreach organization. We should not merely wait for these relationships to miraculously and spontaneously materialize, but we should work to establish them. Secondly, we should receive the encouragement given to us in these relationships without question or suspicion. Once again, a problem with low self-esteem can lead us to be mistrustful of others' affection for us. We should lay such mistrust aside. It is wrong for us to reject the love of our brothers and sisters in the Lord.

The Lord wants to help us directly in our battle with low self-esteem. However, he also wants to help us by using other human beings as his instruments. The love of God can come to us in many ways. We should not reject the love of our brothers and sisters—we may find in the end that we are rejecting the love of our Heavenly Father.

Humility

The principle of truth governs the first act of repentance: We reject lies about ourselves by believing the truth. The second part of repentance—the rejection of self-pity and self-preoccupation—is governed by another principle. This is the principle of humility. As we have seen, humility means serving others, putting others first, laying aside concern for oneself and one's own interests, and taking up a concern for others. False humility only reflects and intensifies problems with low self-esteem. However, true Christian humility is one of the best weapons we have to use against these problems.

By turning our attention toward others, Christian humility liberates us from the introspective patterns of thought that often accompany low self-esteem. As we forget about ourselves, the Lord is able to care for us in a more direct way. I have seen this dynamic operating in the life of a young woman I know. She had suffered in the past from severe depression, discouragement, and self-hatred. Whenever the circumstances of her life gave her a chance to be preoccupied with her problems, she would quickly get ensnared in their web. Then she took a job caring for the practical needs of a group of disabled adults. This job began a major change in her life. She started to forget about her own problems and to take responsibility for the special needs of those who were now in her charge. Her problems did not go away; she still suffered from emotional instability. But the need to serve others helped her to gain a new level of strength and confidence in dealing with these problems.

This principle of humility is also important because it complements the principle of encouragement. Some people with low self-esteem are almost too eager to receive encouragement from others; they engage in a desperate search for acceptance, love, and encouragement. When people search for love from a self-centered orientation, their desires are usually frustrated. They are never satisfied with the imperfect love they inevitably receive, and their intense desire for approval and affection makes others uncomfortable. A self-centered search for encouragement will only deepen problems with self-esteem. However, if one develops personal relationships in Christian humility—from a desire to serve others and not simply to receive from them—then these relationships will prosper and bring genuine encouragement and love.

In my experience as a pastor, I have found that many dissatisfied, insecure people live on the fringes of Christian churches, prayer groups, fellowships, and communities. These people complain regularly about how poorly their needs are met. They say: "This is supposed to be a group of Christians! No one ever calls me, or visits me, or takes an interest in me. I have many needs, and I'm not being properly cared for. Something needs to change!" These people often see some genuine weaknesses in their Christian groups. Christians often fail to care for one another as they should. Furthermore, some of the people who complain this way are objectively needy people who require more help than they are currently receiving. At other times, however, insecure people who talk this way are merely indulging themselves in an entirely self-concerned existence. They overlook the many ways in which people in their groups have tried to reach out to them, or they view these attempts as half-hearted and unworthy. They make no effort to fulfill anyone else's needs. In this case, the main thing that should change is themselves. "Look outside yourself, and serve your brothers and sisters. Then you will find that your own needs are better provided for."

We can now see that Christian humility is not only a virtue in its own right, but also an essential positive principle in the strategy for overcoming low self-esteem.

Patience

Patience is an important quality needed to overcome any formidable personal problem. Difficulties that are deeply rooted in our personalities do not change overnight. They develop over much time, and they can only be uprooted over time.

I had to confront this human reality when I started to deal with a personal difficulty in the area of anxiety. Early in my life as a Christian I realized that I had a problem with anxiety and intensity. I prayed that God would free me from this problem. I hoped that he would take it away quickly, but I was willing to have him change it over a longer period of time—say, over the course of one year. Then I discussed the problem with an older and more experienced Christian friend. He laughed when I told him that I was patient enough to work on my anxiety for a year. "I'm sure you'll make great progress over the next year," he said, "but if you expect the problem to be fully overcome then, you will probably be mightily discouraged. To be realistic, I think you should plan to work on the anxiety problem for at least the next five to ten years." This remark left me almost speechless. Five to ten years! For a man who has only lived twenty years or so, ten years seems like an interminable length of time.

Nevertheless, I soon adapted to this new time perspective. In fact, the long-range view gave me a sense of peace that I had not experienced before; I became less anxious about my anxiety when I recognized that the problem would be with me for a while. I was able to learn how to live with it and around it. At the same time, I knew that I could expect significant improvements as the years passed. The importance of faith and patience now became especially clear to me.

Patience is particularly important for someone who is combatting low self-worth. The problem itself is usually associated with discouragement. Many things make an insecure person discouraged, including obstacles to his or her efforts to change. The temptation is to grow weary and disheartened when the problem does not totally yield to the first or second assault. At this early point in the battle, the Christian's armor consists of patient endurance based on faith in God's goodness and power, and hope in his promises.

This warfare imagery illustrates a final point about patience—it is an active rather than a passive virtue. In fact, the word "perseverance" better captures the essential meaning of the New Testament word usually translated as "patience." An example from ancient warfare will help us here. Most ancient emperors of great power—such as Nebuchadnezzar, Alexander of Macedon, and the indomitable Romans—made war by laying siege to a leading city that resisted them. Sometimes the siege would last from five to ten years, but eventually the enemy would be starved and the walls breached. The victory would come through perseverance. Similarly, it is not enough to simply sit and wait for our problem with self-worth to magically disappear with the passage of time. Instead, we must actively "lay siege" and fight to overcome it.

Prayer

Our seventh and final principle is one of the most important: the principle of prayer. God is not distant and remote, unconcerned about the problems we face in our lives. Instead, as the psalmist writes, "The Lord is near to all who call upon him, to all who call upon him in truth. He fulfills the desire of all who fear him, he also hears their cry, and saves them" (Ps 145:18-19). Trusting in the infinite power and goodness of our God, we should offer our every need to him, expecting that he wants to care for us.

What precisely should we pray for? We can pray for confidence, strength, and boldness. We can pray for the ability to reject lies and lay hold of the truth about ourselves. We can pray for divine assistance in our practice of Christian humility. We can pray that the Lord would directly change us by the power of his Holy Spirit so that we can serve him in freedom. We can pray that the Lord would give us further wisdom about what we can do to change. All of these things, and many others like them, are excellent topics for prayer.

Nonetheless, we must always take care that our prayer not begin to revolve around ourselves. This is a pitfall of any personal request in prayer. We begin by sincerely praying to God, the King of the Universe who is worthy of all worship, and we end up wrapped in intense thought about *our* problem. The center of our prayer should always be the Lord himself, not us and our problems. Still, the Lord does want us to present the problems to him, but in faith, reverence, and with eyes fixed attentively on him.

It is also helpful to have others pray for us. We should share our difficulty with those closest to us (rather than with a large group), and ask them to seek the Lord for us. The prayer of God's people has great power. We should remember the promise Jesus made to his disciples: "If two of you agree on earth about anything they ask, it will be done for them by my Father in heaven" (Mt 18:19).

Conclusion

These seven principles together make up a successful strategy for overcoming problems with self-worth. Applying this strategy should help us significantly in our battle. Of course, there will still be a battle to fight; the struggle will not be won without serious opposition. Problems with self-image can be formidable foes. However, the Lord's power and the Lord's wisdom are able to prevail. One should begin the fight with the confident hope of victory.

In these seven guidelines we have emphasized what *we* need to do in order to get free of low self-worth. However, this should not give the impression that the struggle is simply a matter of setting ourselves free. Rather, our task is a matter of fully appropriating the freedom that Christ has purchased for us. God is working in us through the Holy Spirit, and his grace is the source of all our victories. In the final analysis, the most important thing required of us in gaining our freedom is the exercise of faith that opens the door to God's power. There is no substitute for basic faith in Christ and the transforming power of God.

SEVEN

The Goal: Freedom and Servanthood

We have now met the three goals which we set at the beginning of this book: to define Christian humility and distinguish it from a poor self-image and timidity; to describe what our self-image should be as Christians; and to offer practical advice on how to overcome problems with a poor self-image. One question remains: What is the purpose of all this teaching? What might the Lord want to accomplish in us through it? I am convinced that the goal of this teaching on humility and self-worth can be summed up in two words which appear contradictory but which in fact have an important connection: freedom and servanthood.

Freedom

Personal freedom is one of the main goals of this teaching. It is something we can expect. As an expression of his love for us in Christ, God wants to free us from our bondage to problems with self-image and lack of confidence.

In the New Testament, "freedom" is an important word. It describes an essential aspect of our full inheritance in Christ as God's children. "For freedom Christ has set us free; stand fast therefore, and do not submit again to a yoke of slavery" (Gal 5:1). As the people of Israel were redeemed and liberated from bondage to their Egyptian oppressors, so we have been redeemed from the world, sin, Satan, death, and the Law. In the Gospel of Luke, Jesus inaugurates his ministry in Nazareth by reading an important Old Testament passage on freedom and proclaiming that the passage is fulfilled in himself:

> And he stood up to read; and there was given to him the book of the prophet Isaiah. He opened the book and found the place where it was written:
> "The Spirit of the Lord is upon me,
> because he has anointed me to preach good news to the poor.
> He has sent me to proclaim release to the captives
> and recovering of sight to the blind,
> to set at liberty those who are oppressed,
> to proclaim the acceptable year of the Lord."
> And he closed the book, and gave it back to the attendant, and sat down; and the eyes of all in the synagogue were fixed on him. And he began to say to them, "Today this scripture has been fulfilled in your hearing."
> (Lk 4:17-21)

Thus, the mission that Jesus was sent to accomplish is a mission of redemption and liberation.

The problems that we have been discussing in this book hold many Christians in bondage. Insecurity, poor self-image, lack of self-confidence, and timidity—all can rule as merciless taskmasters. They control us, preventing us from living our lives as the Lord would want us to. Satan uses these problems to diminish our joy and fruitfulness, and to frustrate our attempts to grow in the Christian life. Certainly it is no exaggeration to talk about these patterns in terms of bondage and slavery.

The Lord wants to free us from the rule of these problems. The redemption we have in Christ Jesus can permeate our entire lives and bring us to full personal freedom. This does not mean that we will arrive at the place where we witness the disappearance of all our emotional difficulties. It does mean that we can obtain freedom from the domination of these difficulties. The Lord wants to free us from their control so that we can live fully for him.

What is the goal of this teaching on self-image and humility? Part of the answer is that we live in freedom. We live in the power of the Holy Spirit as children of God; free from bondage to timidity, insecurity, a poor self-image, and lack of confidence; experiencing the joy of God's kingdom, living fully for the praise of his glory.

Servanthood

God's intention in freeing us from bondage is always deeper than it seems at first. The people of

Israel danced and sang and rejoiced greatly after the Lord delivered them from Egypt and brought them through the Red Sea; but the redeeming act of God was not complete until forty years later when they were planted in the promised land, having received the Law and the Covenant. God not only intends to free us *from* something, he also wants to free us *for* something.

What is it that the Lord wants to free us for? In a certain sense, it is the same purpose for which he freed the people of Israel from Egypt: to live as his servants and be his people. Our redemption is actually a transfer from one master to another. Paul puts it this way:

> When you were slaves of sin, you were free in regard to righteousness. But then what return did you get from the things of which you are now ashamed? The end of those things is death. But now that you have been set free from sin and have become slaves of God, the return you get is sanctification and its end, eternal life.
>
> (Rom 6:20-22)

The old master was harsh, cruel, and seeking only evil for us. The new master is just, merciful, and eager to give us all good things, including an intimate and privileged relationship with himself.

There is also another aspect to this freedom that the Lord has given to us. First and foremost, this freedom allows us to live as his servants. But secondly, this freedom allows us also to serve one another:

> For you were called to freedom, brethren; only do not use your freedom as an opportunity for the flesh, but through love be servants of one another. For the whole law is fulfilled in one word, "You shall love your neighbor as yourself." (Gal 5:13-14)

Freedom from sin, Satan, death, the world, the Law, and anything else that might separate us from the love of God in Christ Jesus is supposed to culminate in our living as servants in obedience to God and in love to our brothers and sisters. This is the positive freedom given us in Christ: the freedom to live fully for God and his people.

This explains the purpose of much of the Christian teaching on self-image and humility. Freedom from problems with self-image should enable us to live a truly humble life of service. We need no longer be held back from fruitful service by the paralysis of fear, insecurity, and lack of confidence; we need no longer resist the encouragement and admonition of our brothers and sisters in Christ. The Lord wants us to live a life of dedication, service, and love, not looking first to our own interests, but instead looking to his interests and the interests of others. Therefore, he wants to free us from the rule of all those forces which prevent us from living such a life.

The goal of this teaching on self-image and humility is therefore the same as the basic goal of the whole Christian life: to grow in conformity to the image of Christ, abounding in the fruit of the Holy Spirit (Gal 5:22-23), giving glory to God in everything. This is the life made possible by our redemption in Christ. "We are to grow up in every way into him who is the head, into Christ . . . to mature manhood, to the measure of the stature of the fullness of Christ" (Eph 4:15, 13). Christ frees us from servitude to unworthy powers, that we might become, like him, true servants of the One True God.

The books in the Living as a Christian Series can be used effectively in groups. To receive a free copy of the Leader's Guide to this book and the others in the series, send a stamped, self-addressed business envelope to Servant Books, Box 8617, Ann Arbor, Michigan 48107.